YOUR KNOWLEDGE HAS VALUE

The Language of COVID-19 Conspiracy Theories. A Semantic Approach

Lisa Thöne

Bibliographic information published by the German National Library:

The German National Library lists this publication in the National Bibliography; detailed bibliographic data are available on the Internet at http://dnb.dnb.de.

ISBN: 9783389028292
This book is also available as an ebook.

Print and binding: Books on Demand GmbH, Norderstedt, Germany
Printed on acid-free paper from responsible sources.

The present work has been carefully prepared. Nevertheless, authors and publishers do not incur liability for the correctness of information, notes, links and advice as well as any printing errors.

GRIN web shop: https://www.grin.com/document/1474664

University of Paderborn

Department of English and American Studies

Winter Term 2020/21

Seminar: Semantics (B)

The Language of COVID-19 Conspiracy Theories

- A Semantic Approach

Hand-In Date: 13 March 2021

Lisa Thöne

ZfBA Englischsprachige Literatur und Kultur

und Englische Sprachwissenschaft

7th Semester

Table of Contents

1. Introduction

> The main thing that I learned about conspiracy theory is that conspiracy theorists actually believe in a conspiracy because that is more comforting. The truth of the world is that it is chaotic. The truth is, that it is not the Jewish banking conspiracy or the grey aliens or the 12 foot reptiloids from another dimension that are in control. The truth is more frightening, nobody is in control. The world is rudderless (Alan Moore 2003).

These words of the British writer Alan Moore specifically apply to the year 2020 because a global pandemic tests current structures and brings new challenges for all people around the world. Due to this, many conspiracy theories concerning the COVID-19 virus arise and find approval, especially through the quick spread on social media platforms. COVID-19 conspiracy theories threaten science and take advantage of people's fears, existential, psychological as well as physical ones. Language plays a key role in this as it mediates conspiracy theories.

To dissolve and understand the language of conspiracy, it is useful to first look at "single unit[s] of language that [mean] something" – *words*, and their semantic relations within the English language and to the world (OALD). Existing research recognises that conspiracy language is distinct and coins new linguistic structures with new senses which can then insert influence on the recipients which does not serve their cognitive well-being. An example of this would be the extensive use of the word *truth* in conspiracy theories, attached to a narrow belief in the sense of 'the only belief that should be accepted, otherwise, a person will suffer'. If someone is mentally labile and believes that *truth* only refers to that certain narrow belief, the person is likely to be manipulated.

Against this backdrop, this paper deals with the question of which senses are attached to certain words, how these senses relate to senses in non-conspiracy language, the coining of new terminology concerning COVID-19, like for instance the word *plandemic*, as well as the aspect *framing*, which will be explained in the first chapter.

This paper begins by defining the concepts *COVID-19* and *conspiracy*, whereby some further theoretical concepts are included. It will then go on to discuss previous research on COVID-19 and conspiracy. The last section of the first chapter introduces the working hypothesis for the analysis of the semantic structures of COVID-19 conspiracy theories. Next, the data set and the methodology that was conducted to analyse it will be presented. In the second and last section of the second chapter, results like for example patterns, methodological difficulties, and new semantic findings are focussed. Last but not least, the conclusion delivers an overview of all outcomes and their implications.

2. Background/Theory Chapter

2.1 Defining *COVID-19* and *Conspiracy*

According to the Pan African Medical Journal (2020: 1), *COVID-19* is "a novel infectious disease that originated in Wuhan, China in December, 2019 and has spread to many countries". The virus caused a global pandemic, which was declared on 11th March 2020 by the World Health Organization (Pan Afr Med J 2020: 1). This entails not only 14 days of quarantine for confirmed as well as suspected cases, social distancing, and closure of borders of several nations, but also the emergence of many different conspiracy theories around the globe (Pan Afr Med J 2020: 1).

It is necessary here to clarify exactly what is meant by *conspiracy*. The compound *conspiracy theory* is used by the Oxford Dictionary of English (1989-) to refer to "a belief that some covert but influential organization is responsible for an unexplained event". Further on, Areeb Mian and Shujhat Khan (2020) have commented on the term *conspiracy*. In their commentary in the medical journal *BMC Medicine*, Mian and Khan (2020) explain some facts about widespread misinformation concerning the COVID-19 pandemic. Mainly, they assume that the contemporary society of the world is divided (Mian and Khan 2020: 1). This is a precondition for antiscientific groups to form and establish themselves, which is evidenced by over 52 million engagements of conspiracy theory websites in contrast to 100 000 engagements of WHO and CDC websites (Mian and Khan 2020: 1). Mian and Khan (2020: 1-2) mention common themes conspiracy theories deal with and which can be detected on several platforms independently. Focusing specifically on COVID-19 conspiracy theories, Mian and Khan (2020: 1-2) talk about the conspiracy of the virus being "artificially created in a lab by a rogue government with an agenda" and the advice of some conspiracy theorist to take "chlorine dioxide solution", which can be fatal. Furthermore, it is worth to consider the idea that conspiracy theorists usually have some other purpose than to inform, like for instance power interests (Mian and Khan 2020: 2). Nevertheless, this is something that can neither be verified nor falsified. Last but not least, conspiracy theories are immune to criticism (Mian and Khan 2020: 2). Mian and Khan (2020: 1) make aware that the "spread of false information drowns out credible sources and in turn results in further public confusion, ultimately leading to greater spread, and inefficient mitigation of virus transmission". They appeal for transparency, clearness, and honesty of governments (Mian and Khan 2020: 2). Also, they warn of politicising the crisis (Mian and Khan 2). Hereby, Prof. Jonathan Charteris-Black's idea of *framing* (2019) is noteworthy. According to Charteris-Black (2019: 16), continuous representations such as the common themes used by conspiracy theorists introduce some form of cognitive bias because particular aspects of a particular entity or situation are chosen selectively. This can be observed in former president Trump's slogan *Make America great again*. Consequently, *framing* can be imagined as a scale reaching from raising awareness to manipulation, whereby conspiracy theories belong to the field of *manipulation*. The aforementioned quantity of engagement of conspiracy theory websites upholds this because misinformation is accessed excessively (Mian and Khan 2020: 1). Thus, *framing* functions as a tool for conspiracy theorists to make themselves believed and takes on a significant role that will be examined in the analysis part of this paper. Mian and Khan (2020: 2) conclude their commentary by advising "health bodies [to] appropriately manage, educate, and address the people's concerns" because if they do so "there is an opportunity to bridge the level of distrust that has arisen by antiscience movements in recent times".

2.2 Previous Research

Turning now to previous research on the topic of COVID-19 conspiracy theories, the common grounds of this research will be presented. First, researchers agree that COVID-19 conspiracy theories affect the spread of the virus in the world. Such intertwined theories deliver explanations that many people feel are missing in public discourse. This entails that the incitements given by conspiracy theorists to rebel and not implement the virologists' advice and overall regulations are believed and carried out. Already implied in this common ground is the agreement that communication of politicians and the media does not work in so far that the population does not understand further procedures and the reasons for these. Consequently, Shahsavari et al. (2020: 313-4), among others, call for a system which divides up the information on the Coronavirus found on social media, and the news. This should serve to avoid confusion with distinguishing reliable and unreliable pieces of information (Shasavari et al. 2020: 313-4). Lastly, researchers on COVID-19 conspiracy theories consent that the pandemic seeks excessive demands on the levels of healthcare, psychology, communication, and building opinions, among other things. This paper's results should contribute to identify and then systematise words and patterns that are likely to occur in COVID-19 conspiracy discussions and thus to reflect upon those and their implications critically.

On the level of words and patterns of conspiracy theories, Mattia Samory and Tanushree Mitra (2018) have found answers in their research paper *"The Government Spies Using Our Webcams:" The Language of Conspiracy Theories in Online Discussions*. According to them, agents in online conspiracy discussions are "powerful individuals" on the one hand, and "common everyday figures" on the other hand (Samory and Mitra 2018: 19). As another result, Samory and Mitra (2018: 10-2) found vaccines, surveillance, and global issues as common topics of conspiracy theories in general. Moreover, perceived threats, blame, and mistrust are *narrative motifs* found by Samory and Mitra (2018: 12-7). Thus far, all of these findings of conspiracy theories in general correlate with findings of COVID-19 conspiracy theories because Shahsavari et al. identified the following four main conspiracy theories concerning the Coronavirus:

> (i) the virus as related to the 5G network, and Bill Gates's role in a global vaccination project aimed at limiting population growth; (ii) a cover-up perpetrated by the Chinese Communist Party after the virus leaped to human populations based largely on Chinese culinary practices; (iii) the release, either accidental or deliberate of the virus from, alternately, a Chinese laboratory or an unspecified military laboratory, and its role as a bio-weapon; and (iv) the perpetration of a hoax by a globalist cabal in which the virus is no more dangerous than a mild flu or the common cold (2020: 313).

In summary, it was no research found regarding COVID-19 conspiracy theories which closely analysed individual words, their relation to one another and their relation to the world. So far, broad and narrow pragmatic approaches could explain what the effect of COVID-19 conspiracy theory language, respectively COVID-19 conspiracy theory language, is. The investigation of individual words might show how elements of this language cohere. Then, further research can explain which mental processes are involved in COVID-19 conspiracy thinking and what is the best way to contradict that. Hopefully, this creates clarification and prevents such thinking.

2.3 Working Hypothesis

Having discussed previous research on conspiracy theories in general and COVID-19 conspiracy theories, the final section of the Background/Theory Chapter deals with the working hypothesis of this paper. This paper hypothesizes that the meaning conspiracy theorists attach to individual words connected to COVID-19 is explicit and unilateral. So, the conspiracy theorists whose propositions are employed in this paper count in their introspection with emotional senses for COVID-19-words, while excluding other senses and patterns of aligning senses. Last but not least, they restrict themselves to a small set of words.

3.0 Analysis

3.1 Data and Methodology

The data for this paper is taken from *The Coronavirus Corpus* (2020-) on the website *English-corpora.org* as well as some groups on the platforms *Facebook* and *Reddit* who discussed COVID 19 conspiracy theories. A number of studies analysed data from discussion forums on Facebook and Reddit before and could make significant findings. The Coronavirus Corpus data is retrieved from online newspapers and magazines. For the most part, journalists do not themselves write articles that could be categorised as COVID-19 conspiracy theories. Despite this, direct speech of conspiracy theorists can be found. This direct speech was extracted. To proceed, previous research helped as a reference point. Terms like *Bill Gates, microchip, vaccine, World Health Organisation, Elon Musk, Illuminati,* and *New World Order* were shown to be closely connected to the context of COVID-19 conspiracy theories, so these terms were the queries, out of which 100 examples each were sorted manually with *Excel*. The examples from Facebook and Reddit were also *cleaned*, so merely the quotes containing conspiracy thinking were taken over. After this, the sample was transferred to *Antconc*, a tool created by the linguist Laurence Anthony to analyse own corpora with some specific functions. The overall data set consists of 51 phrases and sentences, which split up into 2731 word tokens. This corpus will be called primary corpus in the course of this paper.

After having extracted data from different sources, relevant aspects for analysis were to be considered. These are *sense relations*, distinguishing between and abstract and concrete expressions, as well as determining frequency and quantity. Also, *framing* plays an important role, as mentioned earlier. The overall method used was introspection, to get inspired, to then analyse everything empirically by checking with *Antconc*, the Coronavirus Corpus (2020-) as a reference corpus, and secondary literature on the topic.

3.2 Results

Methodologically, it was difficult to find data in the Coronavirus Corpus. One major drawback of this approach was that this corpus deals with text from usually fact-checked articles. Therefore, this paper oriented on approaches of previous research. The previous study on conspiracy in general by Samory and Mitra (2018) proposed to have a look at subgroups on the online platform *Reddit*. Accordingly, COVID-19 conspiracy discussions of the platforms Reddit and Facebook were taken into account and enriched the primary corpus.

The given data from the data set that was put together can be divided into a few semantic fields. These are medical/health; powerful figures, especially Bill Gates; the world/world population, and system/order/control. Words belonging to these fields appeared about 20 times each. Striking terminology, which for this context means that the terms are products of neologisms, blendings, and abbreviations, so creative linguistic structures, is *plandemic*, *scamdemic*, *gov*, *NWO*, and *shepeople*.

To distinguish between sense relations, collocates of words from the COVID-19 conspiracy corpus were compared to collocates of words from the reference corpus, namely the Coronavirus Corpus (2020-). *Bill Gates* appeared four times directly in the COVID-19 conspiracy corpus. First of all, Bill Gates is claimed to belong to the elite. *Elite/s* appears two times in the COVID-19 conspiracy corpus (2020-). The context hints that it is generally agreed that Bill Gates would be a person in a power position with a systematic plan to expand his power. To interpret the collocates, the discursive context around Bill Gates must be understood. In 2018, he held a presentation predicting a pandemic according to the information in the Coronavirus Corpus (2020-).

Looking further into detail, the blended word *plandemic* occurs in causal relation with people of the *elite* like Bill Gates because the *elite* would have actively planned the pandemic to install microchips and take control. Oxford Languages (2020) released a collection of words from the crisis. They explain that *plandemic* was used first in 2006 to indicate a different sense, namely 'a proliferation of plans' (Oxford Languages 2020: 9). Nowadays it is nearly exclusively used by corona conspiracy theorists, who often refer to the aforementioned video of Bill Gates, especially in the COVID-19 conspiracy corpus, and spread misinformation about the disease (Oxford Languages 2020: 9). Accordingly, collocates of *plandemic* in the primary corpus are *agenda, corrupt, elites, fake, fraud, hidden, order* (cf. *New World Order*), *scamdemic, plandemic, truth,* and *world.* All of these appear one time. Oftentimes, words with synonymous meanings like *they/them* are used for such words as *elite.* The sense of *plandemic* derived from the collocates is 'a pandemic planned by elitist people who withhold it from the public'. Similarly, but not so strikingly, the term *scamdemic* occurs in the COVID-19 conspiracy corpus. In contrast to the sense of *plandemic* in the primary corpus, this term was used by the mainstream media to discuss the sense that conspiracy theorists attach on a meta-level. In the reference corpus, the sense of *plandemic* is 'videos of COVID-19 conspiracy theorists who claim that the pandemic was planned by elitist people who withhold that from the public'. For example, the reference corpus refers to a "26-minute video called "Plandemic: The Hidden Agenda Behind Covid-19"" (Coronavirus Corpus 2020-).

Moreover, rather neutral words collocate *Bill Gates* in the reference corpus. Collocates of *Bill Gates* in the Coronavirus Corpus (2020-) are *Microsoft*, with 519 to over 3000 instances of *Bill Gates, co-founder*, with 281 instances, *billionaire*, with 252 instances, *founder*, with 229 instances, and *philanthropist*, with 201 instances. These are words belonging to the semantic fields *economy, work,* and *character.* Thus, the sense of Bill Gates in the reference corpus is 'a friendly, economically successful person'. However, Bill Gates is also often collocationally connected to *conspiracy* and *vaccines*, but again, these words are used for a discourse on a meta-level. In addition to these findings, the collocate *warned* appeared 75 times because Bill Gates for example "warned of Chinese super virus in 2018" and "warned that coronavirus in Africa could overwhelm health services" (Coronavirus Corpus 2020-). Consequently, the word *Bill Gates* is a polysemy with antonymous meanings when looking at the two corpora. A notable example is the sense 'warning' in the reference corpus, whereas the sense 'planning' occurs in the primary corpus. In the reference corpus *warning* means 'passively trying to prevent a catastrophe' and in the primary corpus *planning* means 'actively elaborating an evil plan'. Löbner (2013: 214) distinguishes between different types of antonymies. Referring to his theory, one could either argue that *warning* and *planning* in the aforementioned senses are complementaries or heteronyms. Löbner (2013: 214) theorises that complementaries are "either-or alternatives within a given domain" like for example "even/odd", "girl/boy", and "voter/non-voter". If there was no evil plan, then nobody could warn of it, thus the relationship could arguably be classified as complemental. Heteronyms contain "more than one alternative within a given domain" like for example "*Monday/Tuesday* (…)" (Löbner 2013: 214). Arguably, a person could warn of something that is in the process of being implemented, but probably the most dangerous aspect could still be prevented. Then, there would be more than one alternative.

Sheep occurred twice in the COVID-19 conspiracy corpus and *shepeople* occurred once. This is striking due to the high keyness in this corpus. The latter term most probably is used like the more common blend *sheeple*, which is denoted in the OED (1989-). The Oxford English Dictionary (1989-) defines *sheeple* as follows: "*depreciative*. People likened to sheep in being docile, foolish, or impressionable". In the context of Covid-19 conspiracy theories both words, *sheep* and *sheeple*, mean 'humans who are indoctrinated and manipulated', which is an abstract meaning. In the reference corpus (2020-), *sheep* refers to 'a specific kind of animal', while *sheeple* is again talked about on a meta-level referring to COVID-19 conspiracy reasoning. So, the meaning of *sheep* in the reference corpus is concrete. An example for the usage of *sheeple* in the reference corpus would be: "according to which a cabal of paedophiles rules the world and manipulates the " sheeple " (…)" (Coronavirus Corpus 2020-). As well as *plandemic*, the blend *sheeple* is used on a meta-level in the reference corpus and has another sense in the primary corpus. For instance, one person claimed that. Therefore, *sheep* and *sheeple* are polysemous, whereby the senses could be regarded as hierarchical concerning their degree of abstraction and specificity. More specifically, the senses of *plandemic* and *sheep/sheeple* in the reference corpus are hyperonyms and the senses in the primary corpus are hyponyms of the senses in the reference corpus.

Concerning the semantic field *system/order/control* the words *order* and *government* showed significant results. In the reference corpus, *order* is referred to as 'a means to maintain structures that proved positive, whereby court and law supervise it' as the collocates are *stay-at-home*, *executive*, *court* and *law*, which appear over 2000 times each, to 32.495 instances of *order* (Coronavirus Corpus 2020-). This can be exemplified by the phrase "in order to stay safe and healthy" (Coronavirus Corpus 2020-). The primary corpus referred to *order* as 'a means to dissolve structures that proved positive for the citizens because governments have a secret systematic plan to gain more power through oppressing citizens', for example *moving into a new world order – one of totalitarianism* (primary corpus). Collocates here are *world*, 6 times, and one time each: *totalitarianism*, *plandemic*, *agenda*, *collaps*, *corrupt*, and similar terminology, to 6 instances of *order* (primary corpus). Thus, the two senses of *order* have an antonymous relationship, but are not concretely related. The word *governments* means in the reference corpus 'state institutions working collaboratively with other institutions and take on responsibility', exemplified by: "governments worldwide are frantically trying to prevent and control fresh outbreaks" (Coronavirus Corpus 2020-). Collocates in the reference corpus, which appear over 400 times are *state*, *local*, *federal*, and *corporations*, whereby *governments* appears 117765 times (Coronavirus Corpus 2020-). The COVID-19 conspiracy corpus has another sense for this word, which is 'institutions working on an international basis, to implement a dangerous plan, thereby being corrupt'. This can be exemplified by the following group description: "This group is made to expose the truth about this Fake Plandemic New World Order Corrupt Elites/Governments (…)" (primary corpus). Collocates like *world*, *order*, *elites*, and *corrupt*, appearing one time each, underline this (primary corpus). So, this polysemous word has an antonymous relation, but again no concretely definable one.

Lastly, sense relations within the semantic field *medicine/health* are striking. The word *covid* is used in the reference corpus to refer to 'a dangerous illness that is not yet well treatable', for instance in: "efforts to care for COVID patients" (Coronavirus Corpus 2020-). In the other corpus, it is defined as 'an illness, invented as a means to transfer power', as in: "covid passport [is] repackaged for digital id" (primary corpus). This polysemous word also has antonymous senses again, created with the prefix {-un}. The *vaccine* is neutrally defined by the mainstream media as 'positively assessed remedy available from different companies to treat COVID-19', like in: "the Covid vaccines do give you a better chance to resist the Covid virus" (Coronavirus Corpus 2020-). In the COVID-19 conspiracy corpus *vaccine* means 'a dangerous medium, used to insert microchips into human bodies', like for example: "Vaccine to be the carrier for genetic modification chemical" (primary corpus). So, the senses of the polysemous word *vaccine* have antonymous relations, more specifically converse relations according to Löbner (2013: 214) because the vaccine takes on reversed roles in those senses.

The last semantic issue here is *framing*. In total, four metonymies that occur in the primary corpus were particularly interesting and all add up to two broader categories: the elites/ government and their New World Order on the one hand, and the world population or *people* on the other hand. This is a frame that establishes the binary opposition *them versus us*, which entails that 'everything either belongs to an evil plan' or means that 'humans are subordinated to an evil plan'. This can be exemplified by the COVID-19 conspiracy corpus with the proposition that "[s]he doesn't know any better She trusted her government but she just trying to warn people about the vaccine", where *government* stands for 'people with an evil agenda' (primary corpus). Another particular frame concerns metaphors about mental and physical health conditions. They can be found in a large number, eight times. All of these refer to people being in a state where they would not be able to build up their own mind, but they would be manipulated. As a consequence, they would have to believe the conspiracy theorists who claim to know the *truth*. Examples for this are: "the world has gone mad… well madder" and "closed mindset", which in this case means that 'the people do not want to believe the *truth* of the conspiracy theorists (primary corpus).

4.0 Conclusion

The major finding of this research paper is several antonymous relations within the senses of polysemous words. Hereby, every time, COVID-19 conspiracy theories claim that specific people in power conduct an agenda to enhance their power. The Coronavirus would be the medium for this. While the mainstream media show a wide range of collocates for words that have to do with COVID-19 all together, the sample of the primary corpus had a small collocational range for words that have to do with the pandemic. This is mirrored in their framing because COVID-19 conspiracy theorists set up a binary opposition between the world citizens and elites/governments, and use terminology of the semantic field *medicine* to pinpoint their assumptions. Furthermore, they coined new specific terminology like *plandemic* for instance. The quantity and quality of individual words used in COVID-19 conspiracy discussions are noteworthy because the range of words is low, and qualitatively, the words get meanings attached that all correspond to one framework. This framework fits the results of previous studies which state that certain *narrative motifs* of conspiracy language exist because these are explicated and substantiated by senses that are antonymous to those used in mainstream media. Also, they mostly are abstract with an emotional value. Thus, the hypothesis cannot be falsified. The most important limitation of this research lies in the fact that the scope is narrow and the question of how to preserve and restore scientific reasoning on internet platforms such as Reddit and Facebook remains open. Nonetheless, one can start by discussing the meanings of individual words and emphasising that words are interpreted differently. Thereby, the results of this research serve as a reference point for that. The internet and its structures are not yet researched widely, and there is lots of hope that systems evolve that help to identify facts and non-facts. Then, also such happenings as the pandemic and its implications will be better understood and taken more seriously.

Works Cited

A quote by Alan Moore. *Goodreads.com*. Available at: https://www.goodreads.com/quotes/662444-the-main-thing-that-i-learned-about -conspiracy-theory-is (Accessed: March 8, 2021).

Bernard, F. O. *et al.* (2020). "COVID-19: the trends of conspiracy theories vs facts," *The Pan African medical journal*, 35(Suppl 2), p. 147.

Charteris-Black, J. (2019). *Metaphors of Brexit : No cherries on the cake?* Cham, Switzerland: Springer Nature.

conspiracy, n. (1989-). *Oed.com*. Available at: https://www.oed.com/view/Entry/39766?redirectedFrom=conspiracy+theory& (Accessed: March 8, 2021).

Coronavirus Corpus. (2020-). *English-corpora.org*. Available at: https://www.english corpora.org/corona/ (Accessed: March 9, 2021).

Fake Pandemic. *Facebook.com*. Available at: https://www.facebook.com/groups/460394941994045 (Accessed: March 9, 2021).

Oxford English Dictionary. (1989-). *Oed.com*. Available at: https://www.oed.com/view/Entry/276420?redirectedFrom=sheeple (Accessed: March 9, 2021).

Loebner, S. (2013). *Understanding semantics, second edition*. 2nd ed. London, England: Routledge. doi: 10.4324/9780203528334.

Mian, A. and Khan, S. (2020). "Coronavirus: the spread of misinformation," *BMC medicine*, 18(1), p. 89.

Oxford languages word of the year. (2020). *Oup.com*. Available at: https://pages.oup.com/ol/word-of-the-year-2020 (Accessed: March 9, 2021).

Reddit.com. Available at: https://www.reddit.com/r/Coronaconspiracy/ (Accessed: March 9, 2021).

Samory, M. and Mitra, T. (2018). "The government spies using our webcams: The language of conspiracy theories in online discussions," *Proceedings of the ACM on human-computer interaction*, 2(CSCW), pp. 1–24.

Shahsavari, S. *et al.* (2020). "Conspiracy in the time of corona: automatic detection of emerging COVID-19 conspiracy theories in social media and the news," *Journal of Computational Social Science*, 3(2), pp. 1–39.

Word. (2020-). *Oxfordlearnersdictionaries.com*. Available at: https://www.oxfordlearnersdictionaries.com/definition/english/word_1?q=word (Accessed: March 8, 2021).